SONGS
RECORDED BY

FRANK SINATRA

VOLUME 3

MUSIC OF THE STARS

Rare Jazz and Popular Songs from The American Songbook

Produced by **John L. Haag**

Sales and Shipping:
PROFESSIONAL MUSIC INSTITUTE
4553 Rubio, Encino, CA 91436
sales@promusicbooks.com
www.promusicbooks.com

Suggestions and submissions for new products always welcome.

All Of Me

Lyric and Music by
Seymour Simons and Gerald Marks

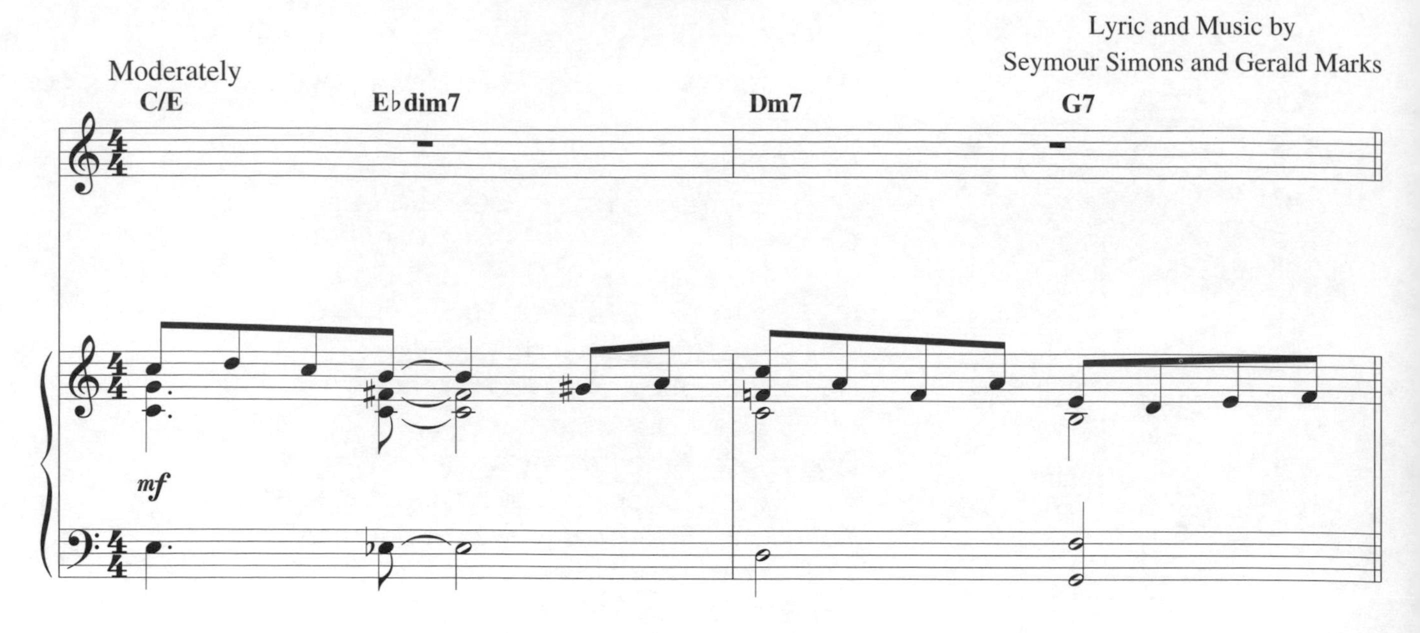

Am7
D7
G7sus4
G7
D9/F♯
Fm6
Fdim7
one - sid - ed love af - fair?
All you took, I
C/E
E♭dim7
Dm
A/C♯
C♯dim7
poco rit.
A♭7
G7
G7+
glad - ly gave. There's noth - ing left for me to save.
Chorus
a tempo
C
E7
All of me, Why not take all of me,
mf
D/F♯
Gdim7
E7/G♯
A7
Adim7
A7
Can't you see I'm no good with -

Dm
E7
- out you.
Take my lips,
I want to lose them,
Am
E+
Cm/E♭
D7
G9sus4
G7
Take my arms,
I'll nev - er use them.
C
E7
Your good - bye
left me with eyes that cry,

D/F♯ Gdim7 E7/G♯ A7 Adim7 A7
How can I go on, dear, with-
Dm F6 F Fm6 Fm
-out you. You took the part that
Em7 Em7♭5 A9 A7 Dm7♭5 G7
once was my heart, So why not take all of
1. C E♭dim7 Dm7 G7+
me.
2. C Fm6 C
me.

A Day In The Life Of A Fool

(Manhã De Carnaval)

English Lyric by Carl Sigman
Original Lyric by Antonio Maria Araujo De Moraes
Music by Luiz Bonfa

G7
Cmaj7
C6
Fmaj7
and hope I'll run in - to the wel - come
E em ca - da cõr bril - hou vol tou o
Bm7♭5
E7♯9
Am
Bm7♭5
E7
sight of you com - ing my way. I
son - ho en - tão ao co - ra - çao. De -
Am
Bm7♭5
E7♭9
Am
Bm7♭5
E7
stop just a - cross from your door, but
- pois des - te di - a fe - liz não
Em7♭5/A
A7♭9
Dm
you're nev - er home an - y - more.
sei se ou - tro di - a ha - ve - a.

Bm7♭5
E7♭9
Am
So back to my room and there in the
E' nos sa a ma - nhã tão be - la a fi -
Bm7♭5
E7
Freely
Am
Dm7
gloom I cry tears of good - bye.
-nal Ma - nhã De car - na - val.
Am
Dm7
Am7
Dm7
Am7
'Til you come back to me, that's the way it will be ev - 'ry
Can - ta o meu co - ra - çao A a - le - gri - a vol - tou tão fe -
Dm7
Em7
a tempo
Am7
Repeat and Fade
day in the life of a fool.
-liz a ma - nhã des - se a - mor.
8va

Chicago

(That Toddlin' Town)

Lyric and Music by
Fred Fisher

C
D7
E♭7
Bet your bot - tom dol - lar you lose the blues in Chi - ca - go, Chi -
Am7
D7
C♯dim7
Dm7
G9
Dm7
G9
Fdim7
- ca - go. The folks who vis - it all wan - na set - tle
Em7
E♭9
Dm7
G7sus
C
Dm7
Em7
A7
down. On State, Street, that great street, I
Dm7
G7
Dm7
G7
A7(♯5)
Dm7
G7
just wan - na say, (just wan - na say,) they do things they

Bm7 E7 Am A7
don't do on Broad - way. Say,
F B♭9 C/E G7(♯5)
you'll have the time, the time of your life. Bring all your friends, your kids
C/E E♭dim7 G7 A♭7 G7
and your wife to Chi - ca - go, Chi - ca - go, my home town.
1.
C Em7 E♭9 Dm7 G7sus
Chi -
2.
C Em7 E♭m6 Dm7 D♭maj7 Cmaj7

Don't Take Your Love From Me

Lyric and Music by
Henry Nemo

Moderately
G+
C
Em7
Cdim
G7
G7-5
G7
Tear a star from out the sky and the sky feels blue, Tear a
take the wings from birds so that they can't fly, Would you
mf

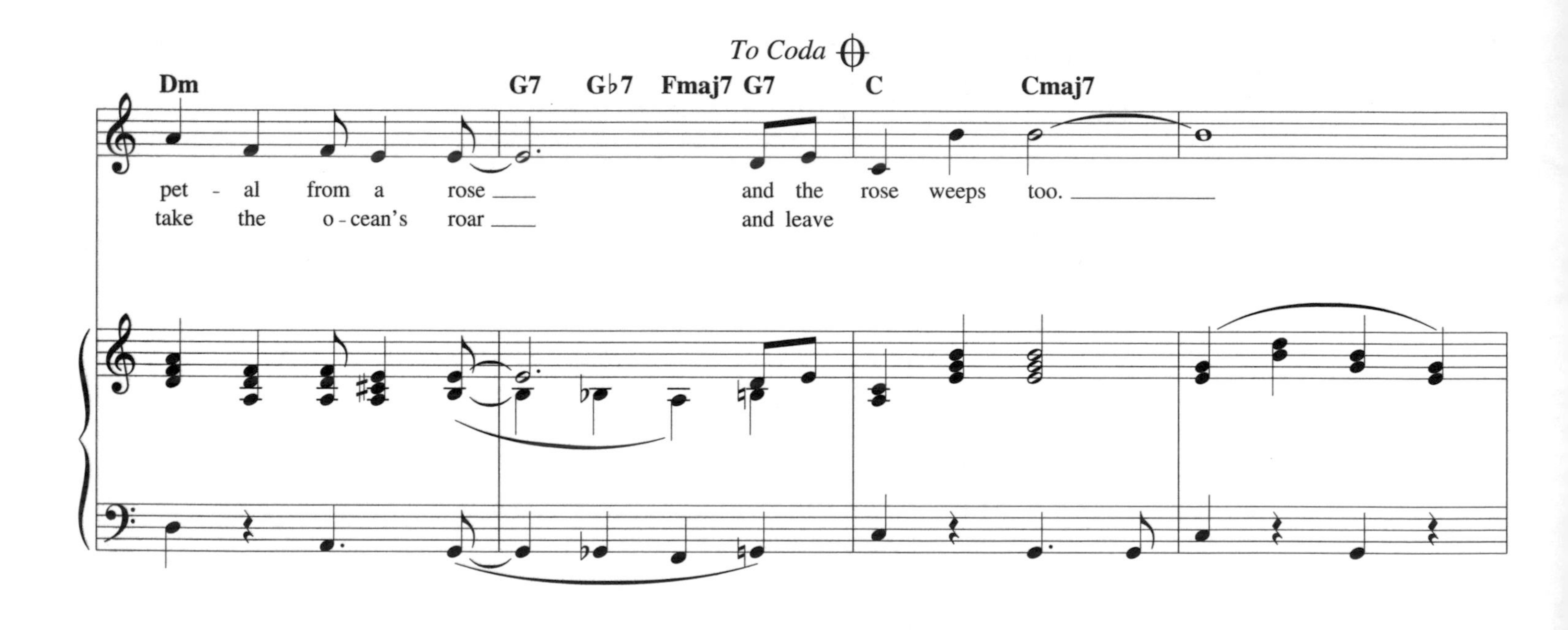
To Coda
Dm
G7
G♭7
Fmaj7
G7
C
Cmaj7
pet - al from a rose and the rose weeps too.
take the o - cean's roar and leave

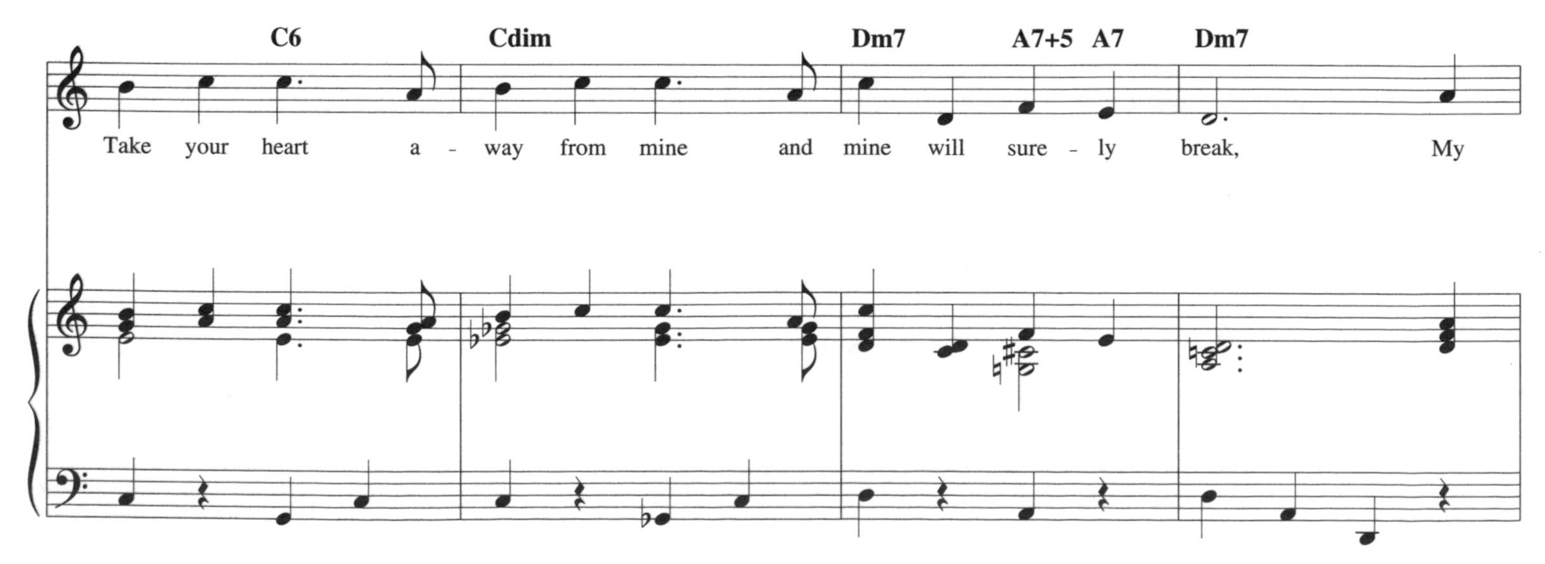
C6
Cdim
Dm7
A7+5
A7
Dm7
Take your heart a - way from mine and mine will sure - ly break, My

D. S. al Coda

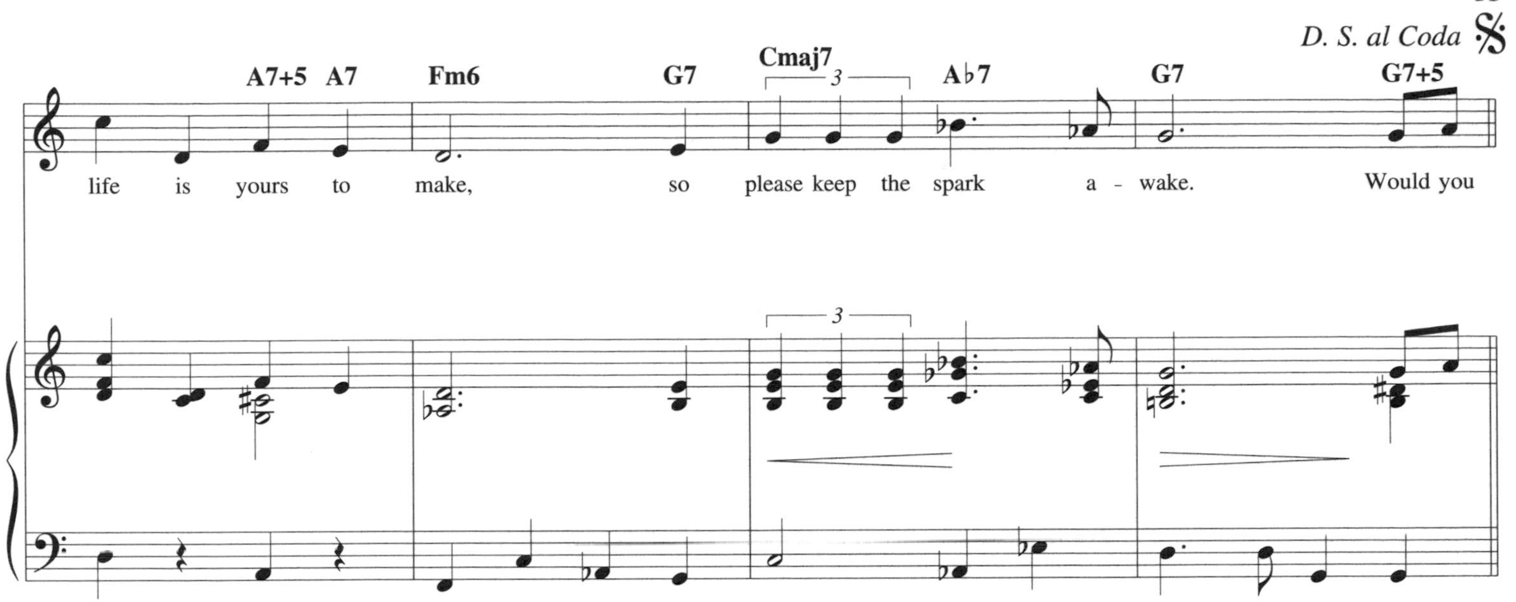
A7+5 A7 Fm6 G7 Cmaj7 A♭7 G7 G7+5
life is yours to make, so please keep the spark a - wake. Would you

Coda
C C7 C7-5 F Fm C
just a sigh? All this your heart won't let you do, This is what I

rit.
Gm6 A7 Dm7 G6 G♭7 Fmaj7 G7 C F Fm C6
beg of you, Don't Take Your Love From Me.

Everybody Has The Right To Be Wrong!

From the Broadway Musical "Skyscraper"

Lyric by Sammy Cahn
Music by Jimmy Van Heusen

G7
Cm
F7
Fm7
B9♭5
B♭9
-part is smil-ing with egg on your face.
E♭
A♭7
Fm7
It's na-ive to make be-lieve that you're right; it's not
B♭7
B9
B♭9
C7
C7♭9
Fm
bright! On-ly fools go walk-ing on thin ice,
Dm7♭5
G7
Cm
Cm/B♭
A♭9
twice! You and life can skip the strife and you'll

E♭/G D♭9 C9 C7♭9 F7♯5 B♭9♯5 E9/B
both get a - long; all it takes is sim - ply say - ing you're
Cm Cm/B♭ F7/A A♭m6 E♭/G E♭dim/G♭ Fm7 E7
wrong when you're wrong, and ev - 'ry - bod - y has the right to be
1. 2.
E♭ D E♭6 Fm7 B9 B♭13 E♭ E♭dim/G♭ Fm7 E7
wrong. it can be a real de - light to be,
E♭ E♭dim/G♭ Fm7 E7 E♭ B♭7 E♭
and I'd fight, fight for the right to be wrong, at least once!

How Little We Know

(How Little It Matters)

Lyric by Carolyn Leigh
Music by Philip Springer

Rhythmically, but not fast

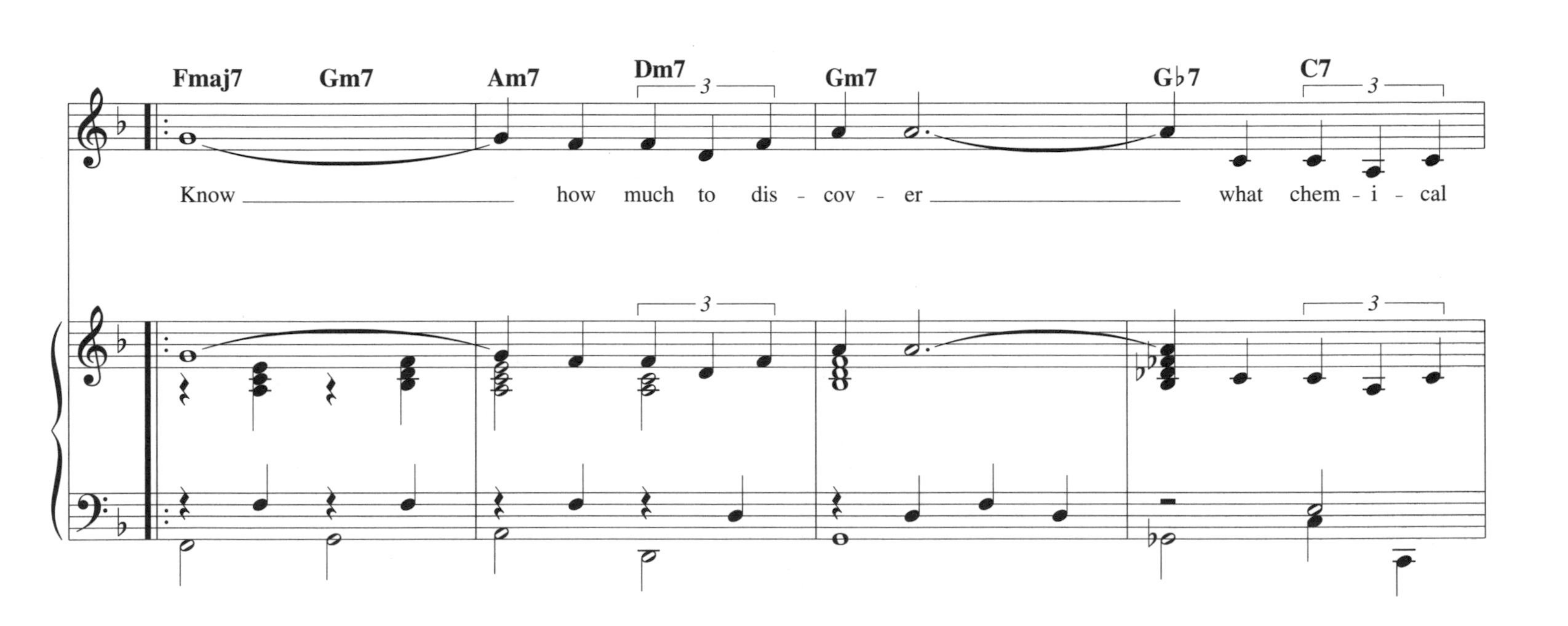

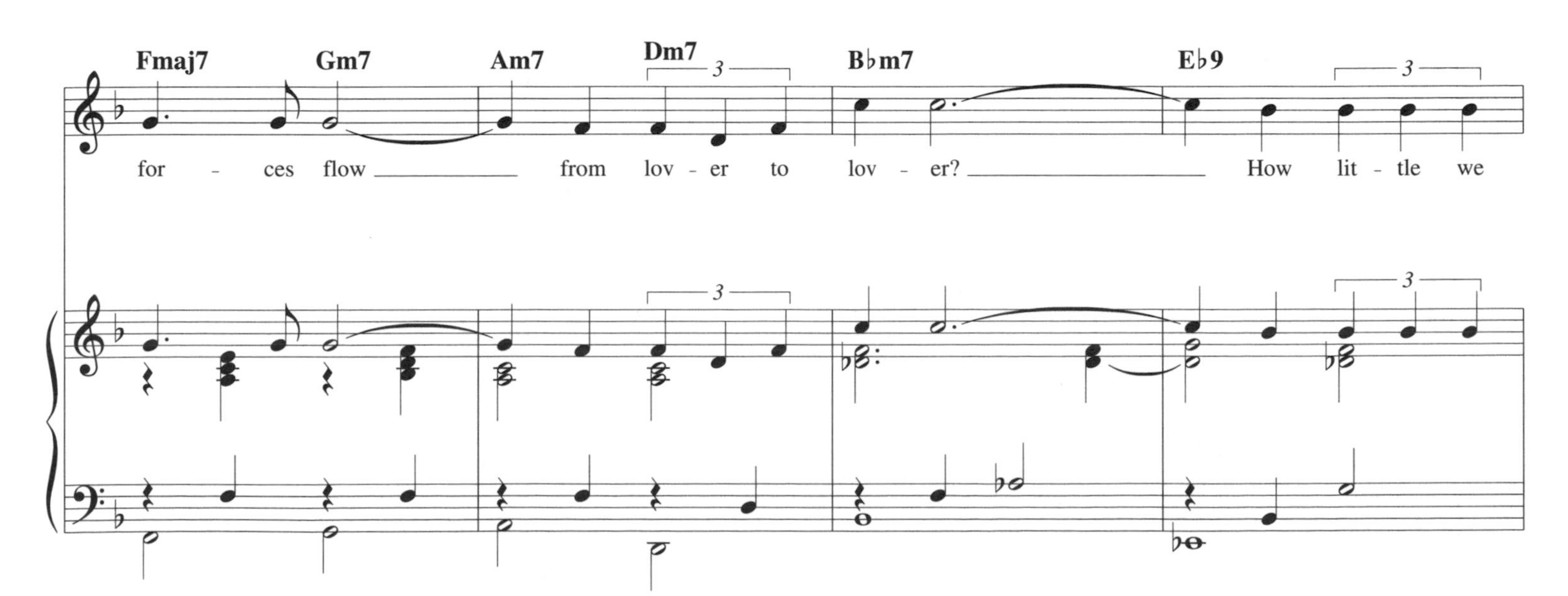

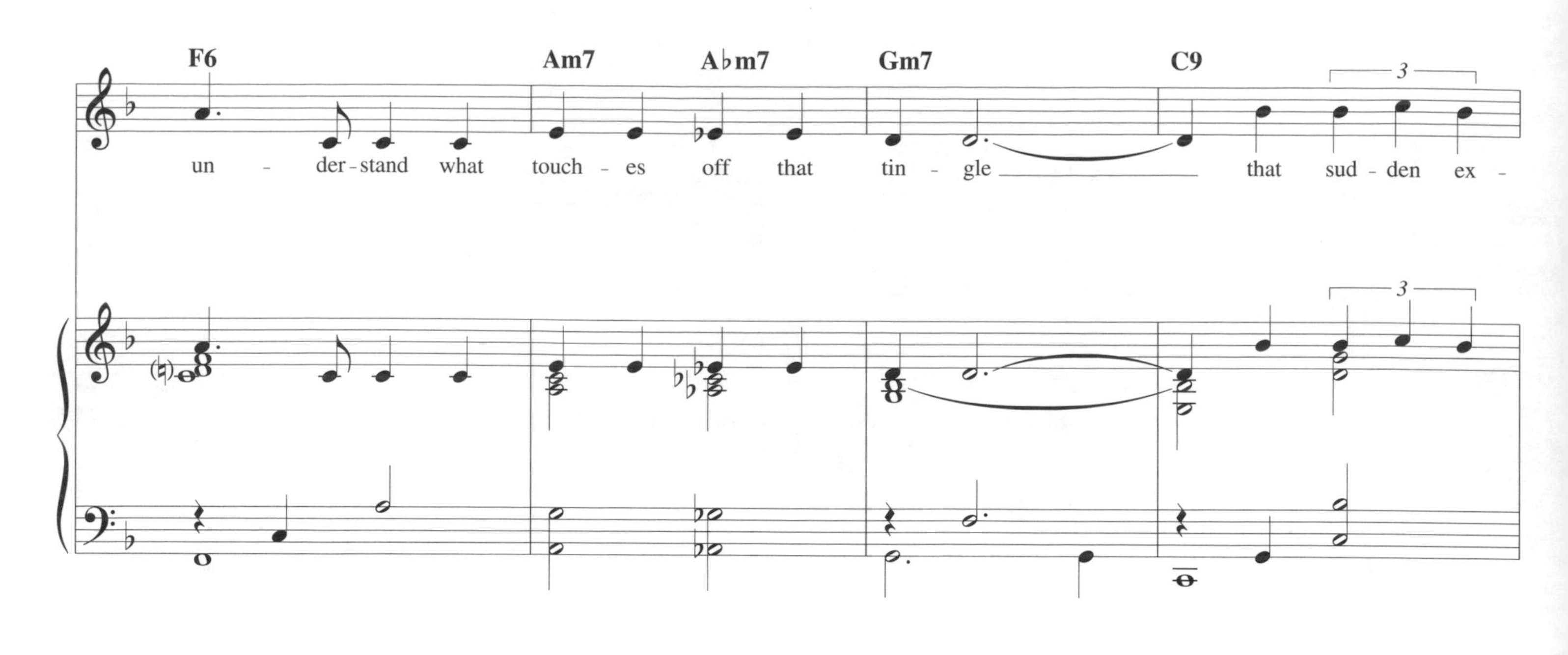
F6
Am7
A♭m7
Gm7
C9
un - der-stand what touch - es off that tin - gle that sud - den ex -

F6
Dm
Am
A♭m7
C7
Fmaj7
Gm7
-plo - sion when two tin - gles in - ter - min - gle. Who cares to de - fine

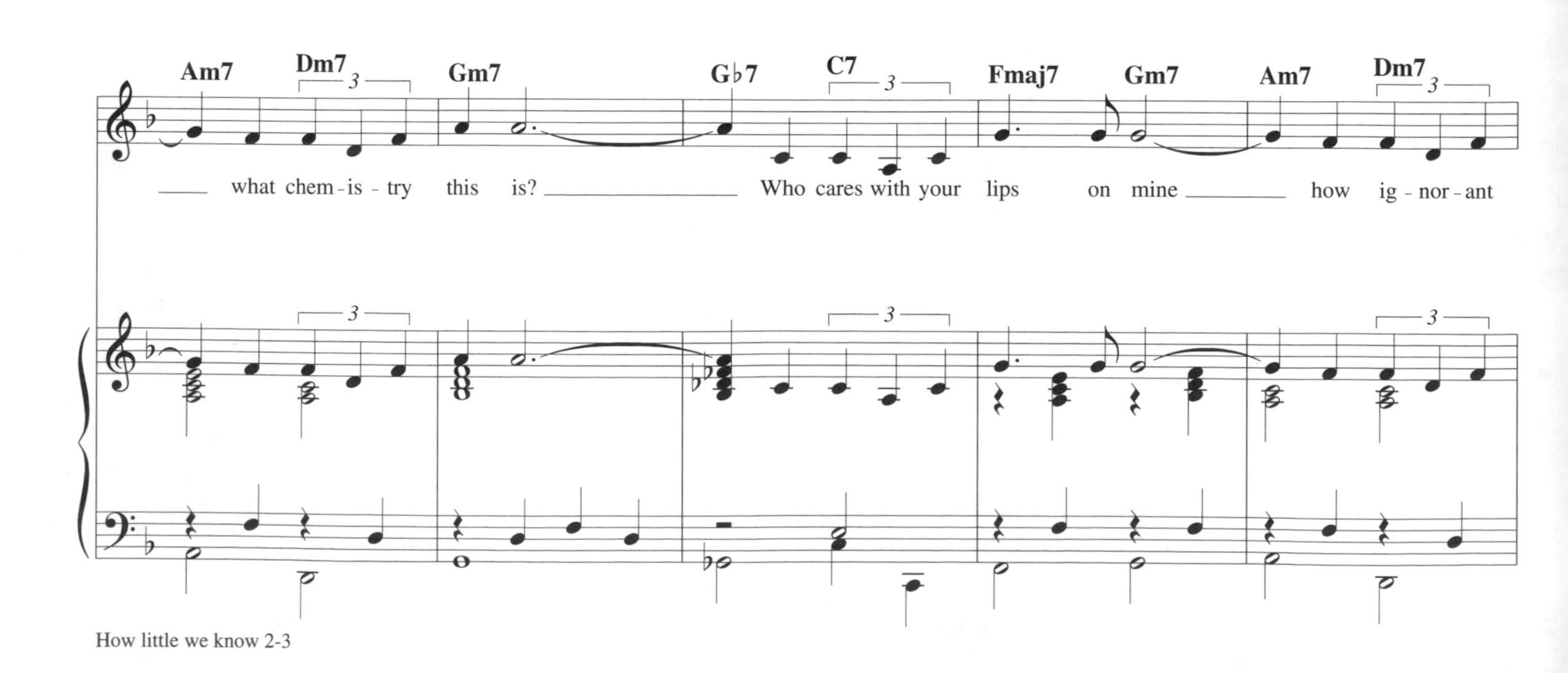
Am7
Dm7
Gm7
G♭7
C7
Fmaj7
Gm7
Am7
Dm7
what chem - is - try this is? Who cares with your lips on mine how ig - nor - ant

B♭m7
E♭9
Cm7
F9
F7-9
bliss is? So long as you kiss me and the world a - round us
Dm7
E♭9
Dm7
Gm7
C7-9
shat - ters How lit - tle it mat - ters, How Lit - tle We
1.
F6
Gm7
C
Know. How Lit - tle We
2.
F6
C9
F6
Know.

I'm Gonna Live Till I Die

Lyric and Music by
Mann Curtis, Al Hoffman and Walter Kent

F♯m7 Am6 B7 B7sus B7 Em
up - side down. I'm gon - na live, live, live till I die.
F♯m7 B7 Em B7 A Dm6 B7
They're gon - na say "What a guy!" I'm gon - na
Em B7 A Dm6 B7 Em B+
play for the sky. Ain't gon - na miss a thing
Em7 F♯m7 Am6 B7 B7sus B7
I'm gon - na have my fling. I'm gon - na live, live, live till I

Em C♯dim Am7 D7 G
die. The blues 'll lay low. I'll make 'em stay low.
Am7 D7 G
They'll nev - er trail ov - er my head. I'll be a
C♯m7-5 F♯7 F♯7-9 G Bm F♯7 B7
dev - il till I'm an an - gel, But un - til then,
Em
Ha - le - lu - jah! Gon - na dance, Gon - na
f
mp

B7 A Dm6 B7 Em B7 A
fly. I'll take a chance rid - in' high.
Dm6 B7 Em B+ Em7 F♯m7 Am6
Be - fore my num - ber's up I'm gon - na fill my cup I'm gon - na
cresc. poco
B7 D7 F♯m D7 B7 B7-9 1. Em B+ Em7
live, live, live, live, live un - til I die.
a poco
ff
Am6 B7 2. Em B+ Em7 Am6 B7 Em
I'm gon - na die.
mp
ff
mp
ff
sfz
R.H.

Isle of Capri

Lyric by Jimmy Kennedy
Music by Will Grosz

F
C7
F
B♭
o - ver,
blue I - tal - ian sky
a - bove.
I said, "La - dy, I'm
a
F
Dm
G7
C7
N.C.
rov - er,
Can you spare a sweet word of
love?"
She whis - pered
p
F
C7
soft - ly, "It's best not to
lin - ger."
And then as
I kissed her hand, I could
see
she wore a
F
C7
F
C7
F
plain gold - en ring on her
fin - ger;
'Twas good - bye on the Isle of Ca - pri.

The Last Dance

Lyric by Sammy Cahn
Music by James Van Heusen

Slowly, smoothly
Abmaj7
Ab7
Ab6
Ab+
Ab
F9
F7b9
last dance, we've come to the last dance.
p - mf
F7
Bb9
Bb7b9
Bb7
They're dim - ming the lights down, They're hop - ing we'll
Bbm7b5
Eb7
Eb7/Db
Ab/C
go. It's ob - vi - ous they're a - ware of us,
C7#5
Fm
Fm7
Bb9
Abm
the pair of us a - lone on the floor; still, I

Eb/G
Cm7
Fm7
Bb7
Bbm7/Eb
Bbm7b5/Eb
want to hold you like this for - ev - er and more.
Eb7
Eb9
Eb7b9
Abmaj7
Ab7
Ab6
Ab+
Ab
It's the last song, they're play - ing the
F9
F7b9
F7
Bb9
Bb7b9
last song. The or - ches - tra's yawn - - - ing;
Bb7
Bbm7b5
Eb7
Eb7/Db
they're sleep - y, I know. They're won - der - ing

A♭/C
C7♯5
Fm
Fm7
just when will we leave,
but till we leave,
keep hold - ing me
B♭7
Bdim7
B♭m7♭5
E♭7
E♭7/D♭
Cm7
F7♭9
tight through the last dance,
each beat of the last dance,
F9
F7♭9
F7
B♭9
B♭7♭9
B♭7
B♭m7♭9
E♭7♭9
and save me the first dance in your dreams to -
1.
A♭6
A♭+
A♭
E♭9
E♭7♭9
2.
A♭6
A♭+
A♭
A♭6/9
- night.
It's the
- night.

My Blue Heaven

Lyric by George Whiting
Music by Walter Donaldson

C7 G♭dim7 B♭7
a lit - tle nest that's nes - tled where the
E♭ Edim B♭7 N.C. E♭
ros - es bloom. Just Mol - lie and me
and ba - by makes three, we're hap - py in
F7 F7(♭5) B♭7 E♭ A♭ E♭
my blue heav - en.

The Lonesome Road

(Popular Version from the Motion Picture "Show Boat")

Lyric by Gene Austin
Music by Nathaniel Shilkret

Dm
Am
Dm
Wear - y to - ten' such a load, Tredg - ing down that
rit.
a tempo
Am
C7
F
B♭m
lone - some road. Look down, look down that lone - some road, Be -
F
C7
F
- fore you trav - - el on.
True
B♭m
F
C7
love, true love, what have I done, That you should treat me

F
B♭m
so? You caus - ed me to walk and talk, like I
F
C7
F
Dm
nev - - er did be - fore. Wear - y to - ten'
Am
Dm
Am
C7
rit.
such a load, Tredg - ing down that lone - some road. Look
a tempo
F
B♭m
F
C7
F
rit.
down, look down that lone - some road, Be - fore you trav - el on.
dim.
8va
8ba

It Was A Very Good Year

Lyric and Music by
Ervin Drake

Moderately
rit.
mf

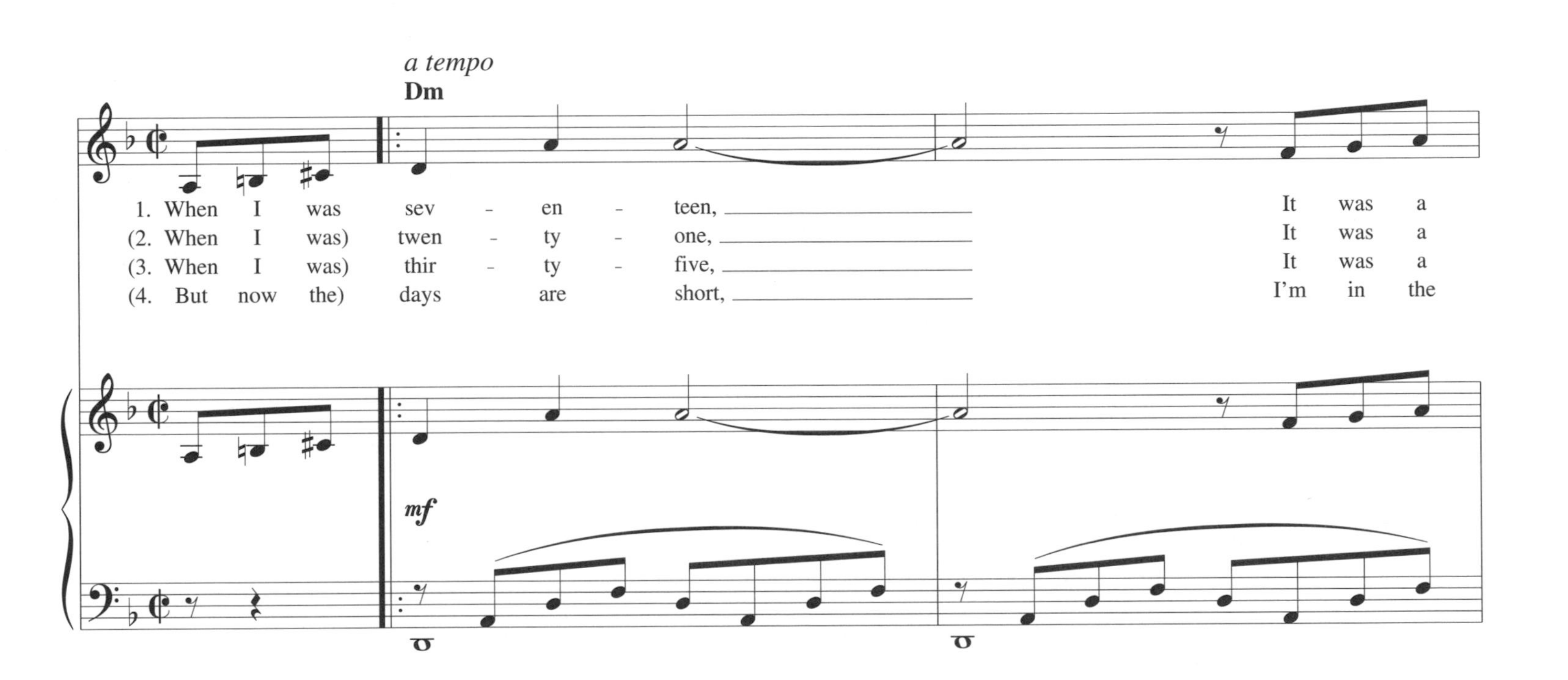
a tempo
Dm
1. When I was sev - en - teen, It was a
(2. When I was) twen - ty - one, It was a
(3. When I was) thir - ty - five, It was a
(4. But now the) days are short, I'm in the
mf

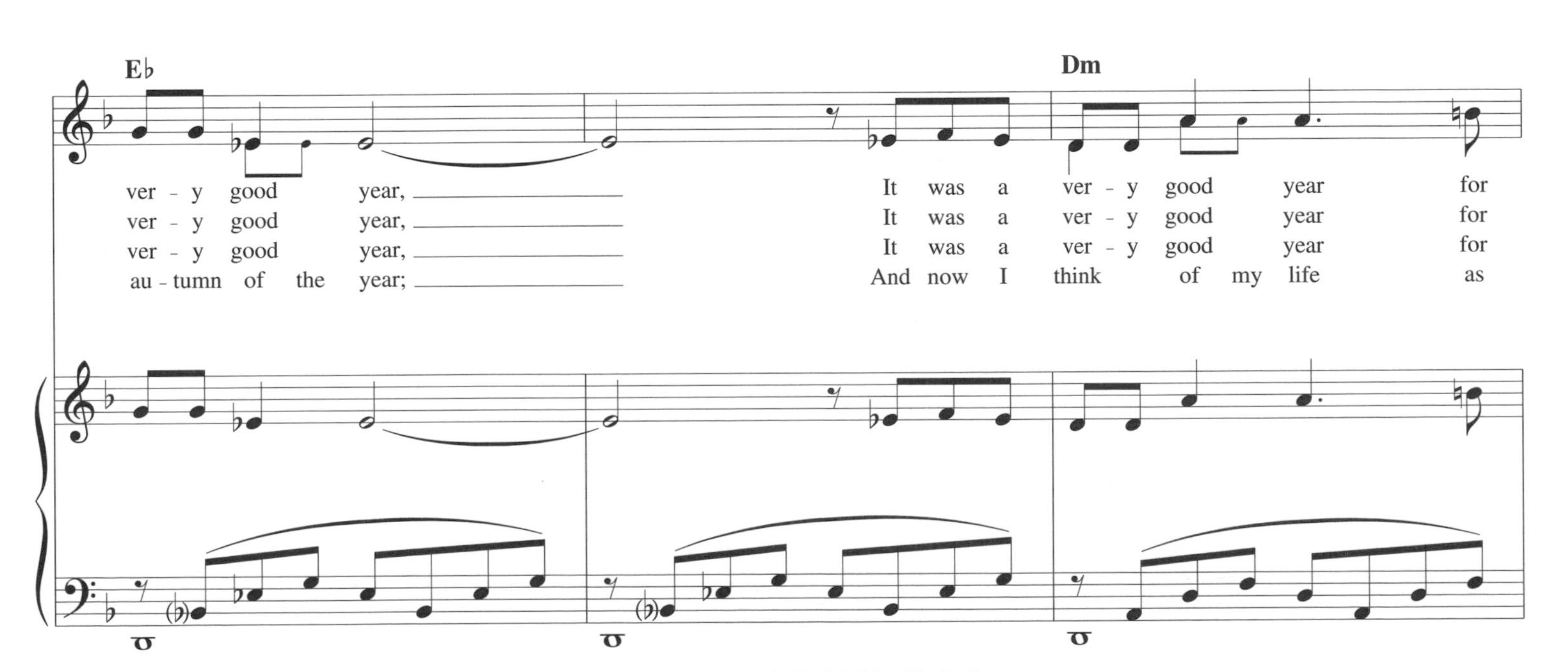
Eb
Dm
ver - y good year, It was a ver - y good year for
ver - y good year, It was a ver - y good year for
ver - y good year, It was a ver - y good year for
au - tumn of the year; And now I think of my life as

F
E♭
small town girls and soft sum - mer nights, We'd
cit - y girls who lived up the stair, With
blue - blood - ed girls of in - de - pen - dent means, We'd
vin - tage wine from fine old kegs, From the

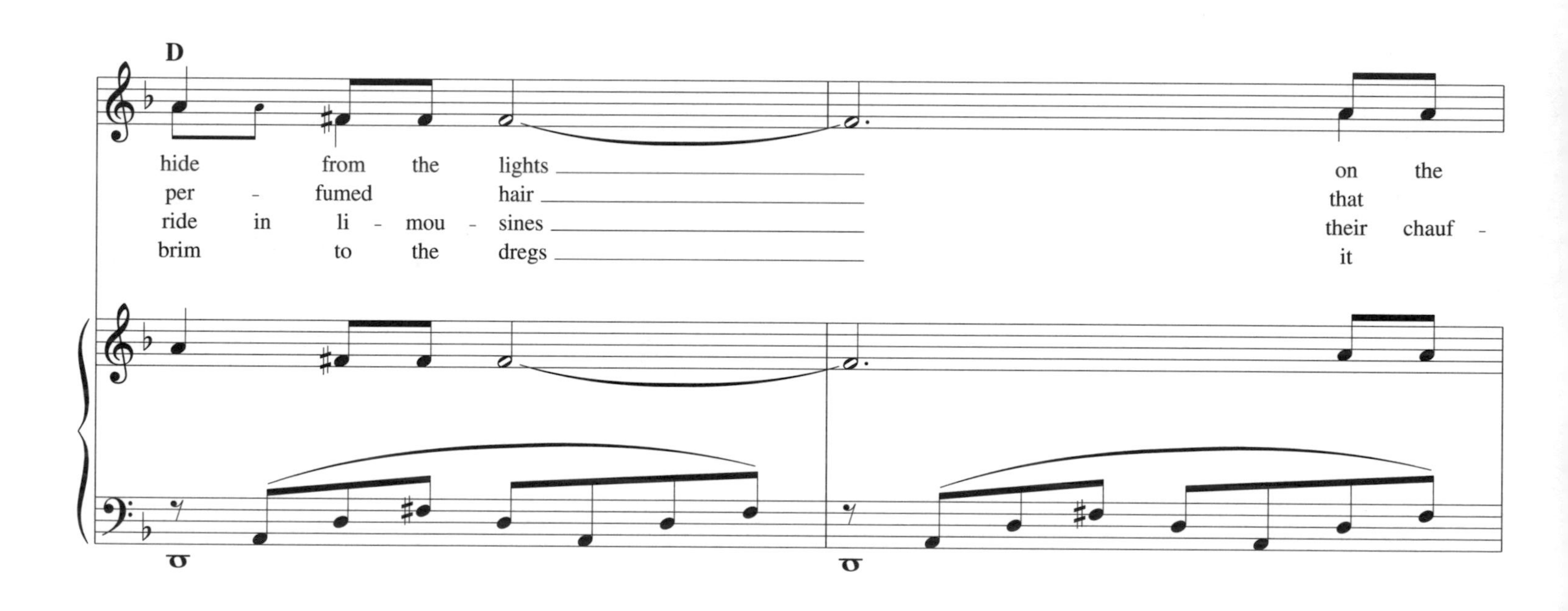
D
hide from the lights on the
per - fumed hair that
ride in li - mou - sines their chauf -
brim to the dregs it

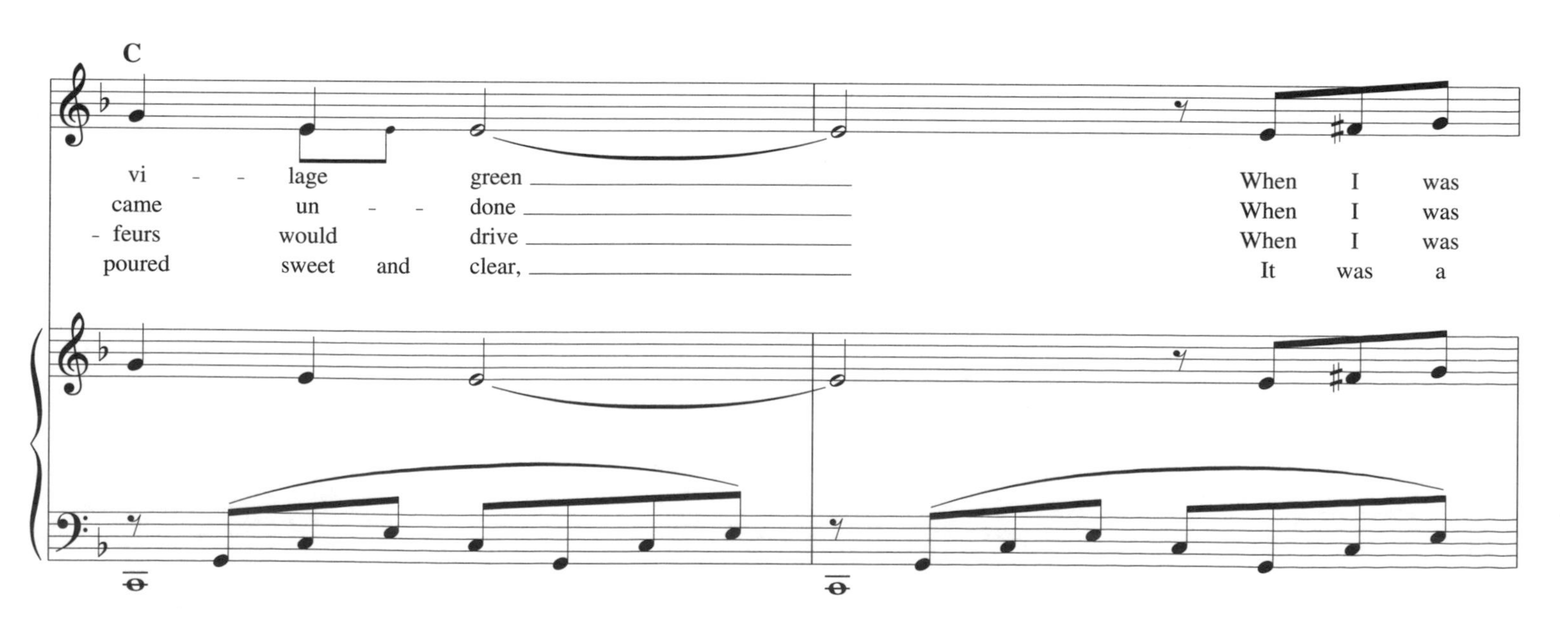
C
vi - - lage green When I was
came un - - done When I was
- feurs would drive When I was
poured sweet and clear, It was a

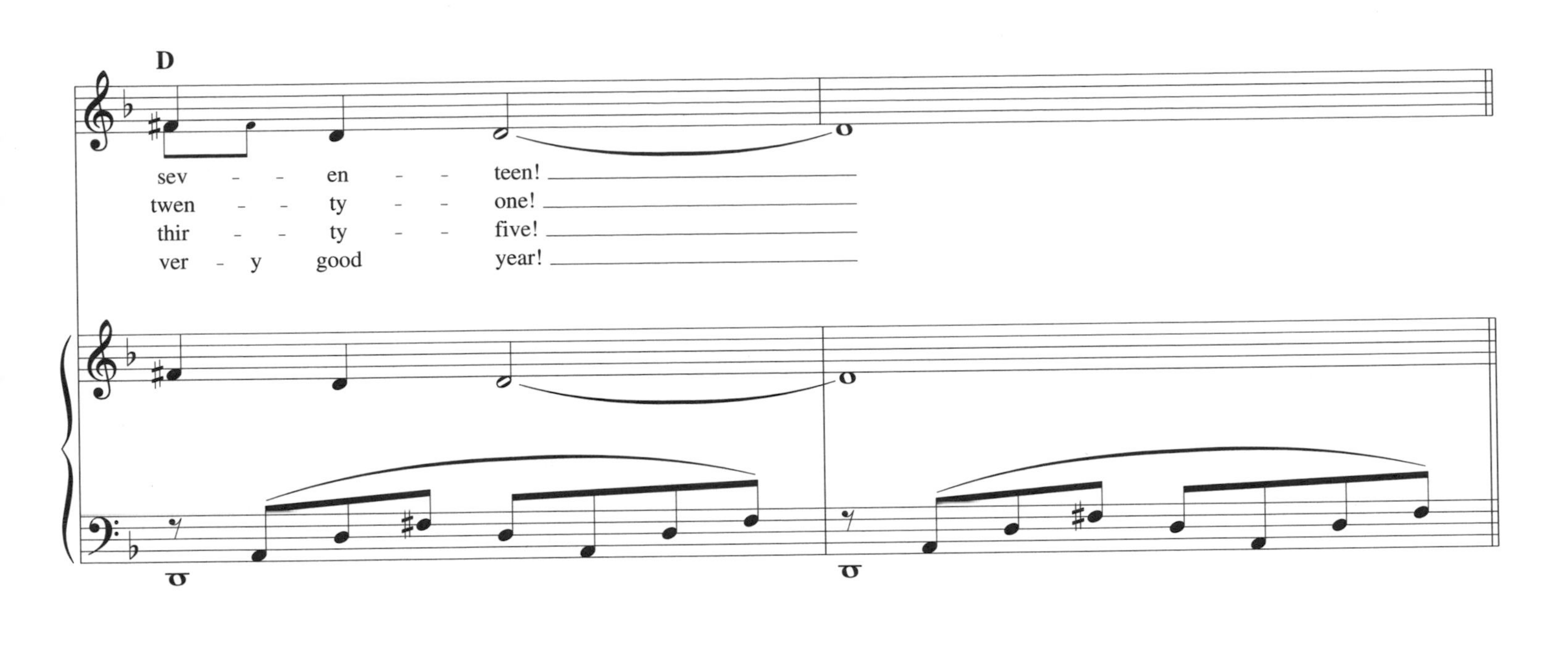
D
sev - - en - - teen!
twen - - ty - - one!
thir - - ty - - five!
ver - y good year!

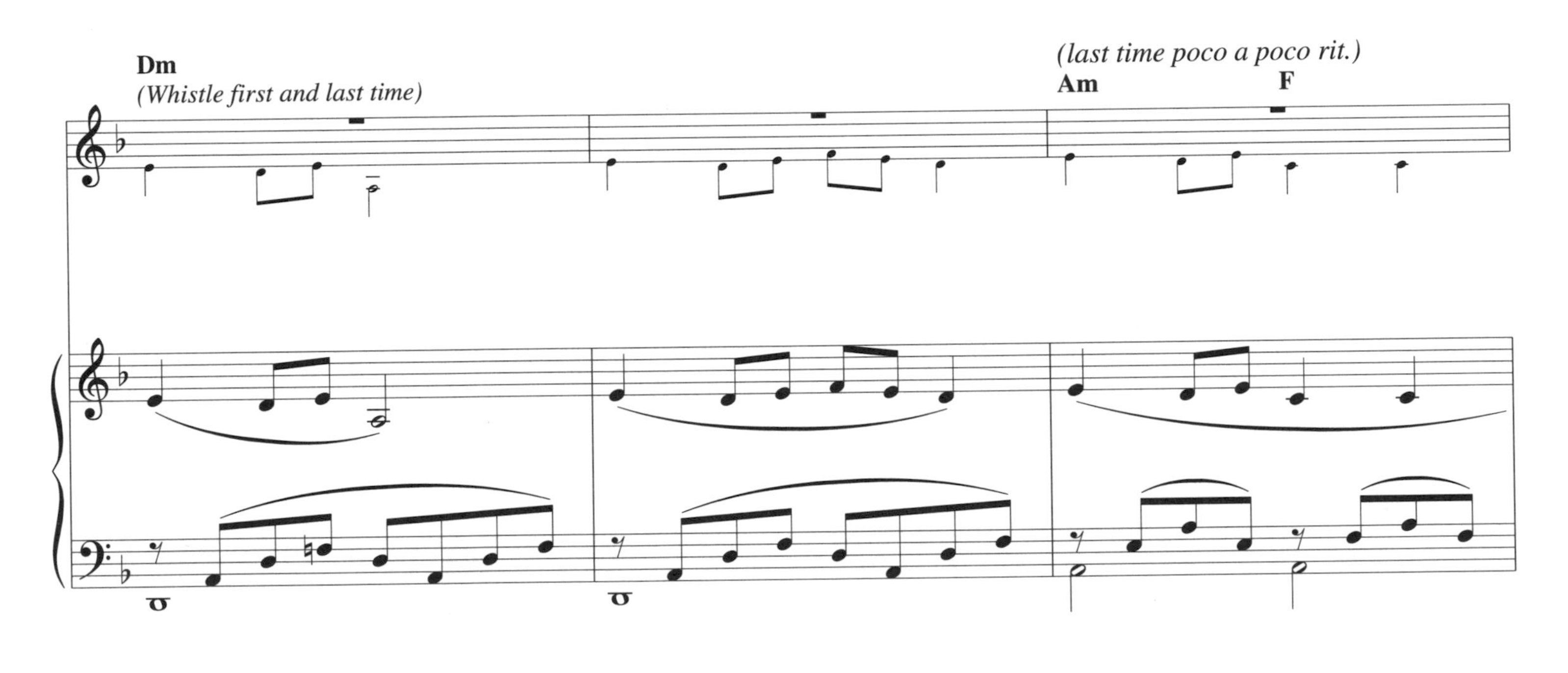
Dm
(Whistle first and last time)
(last time poco a poco rit.)
Am
F

1., 2., 3.
poco rit.
A7
2. When I was
3. When I was
4. But now the
4.
A7
A
pp

Looking At The World Thru Rose Colored Glasses

Lyric and Music by
Tommy Malie and Jimmy Steiger

Moderato
G
G♯dim
D7
Look - ing at the world thru rose col - ored glass - - - es
p - mf

G
B
C
E7
Ev - 'ry - thing is ros - y now,
Look - ing at the

E7
A7
world and ev - 'ry - thing that pass - es,
Seems of ros - y hue some

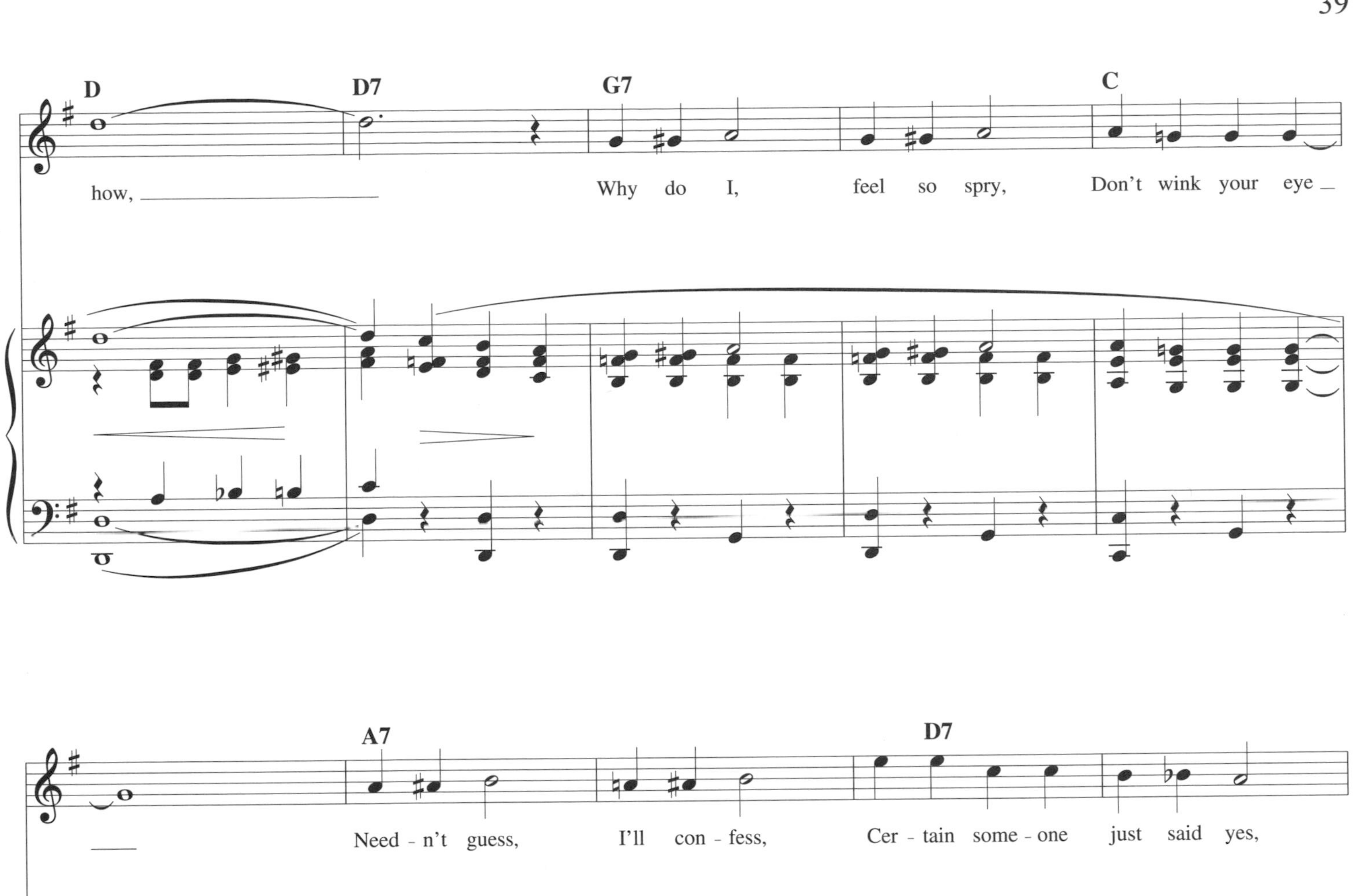
D
D7
G7
C
how,
Why do I,
feel so spry,
Don't wink your eye

A7
D7
Need - n't guess,
I'll con - fess,
Cer - tain some - one
just said yes,

G
G♯dim
D7
In a bung - a - low
all cov - ered with ros - - es,

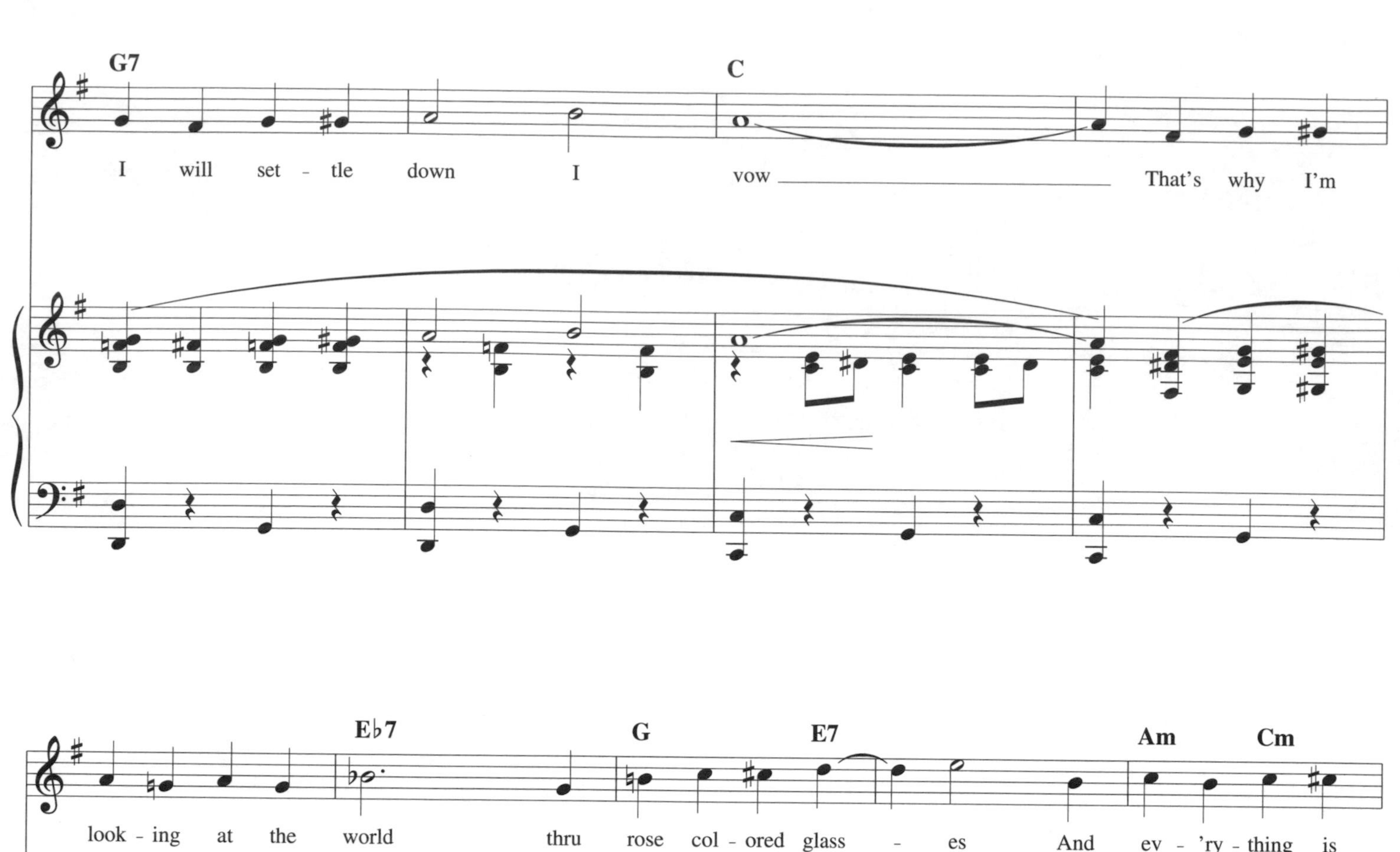
G7
C
I will set - tle down I vow
That's why I'm

E♭7
G
E7
Am
Cm
look - ing at the world thru rose col - ored glass - es And ev - 'ry - thing is

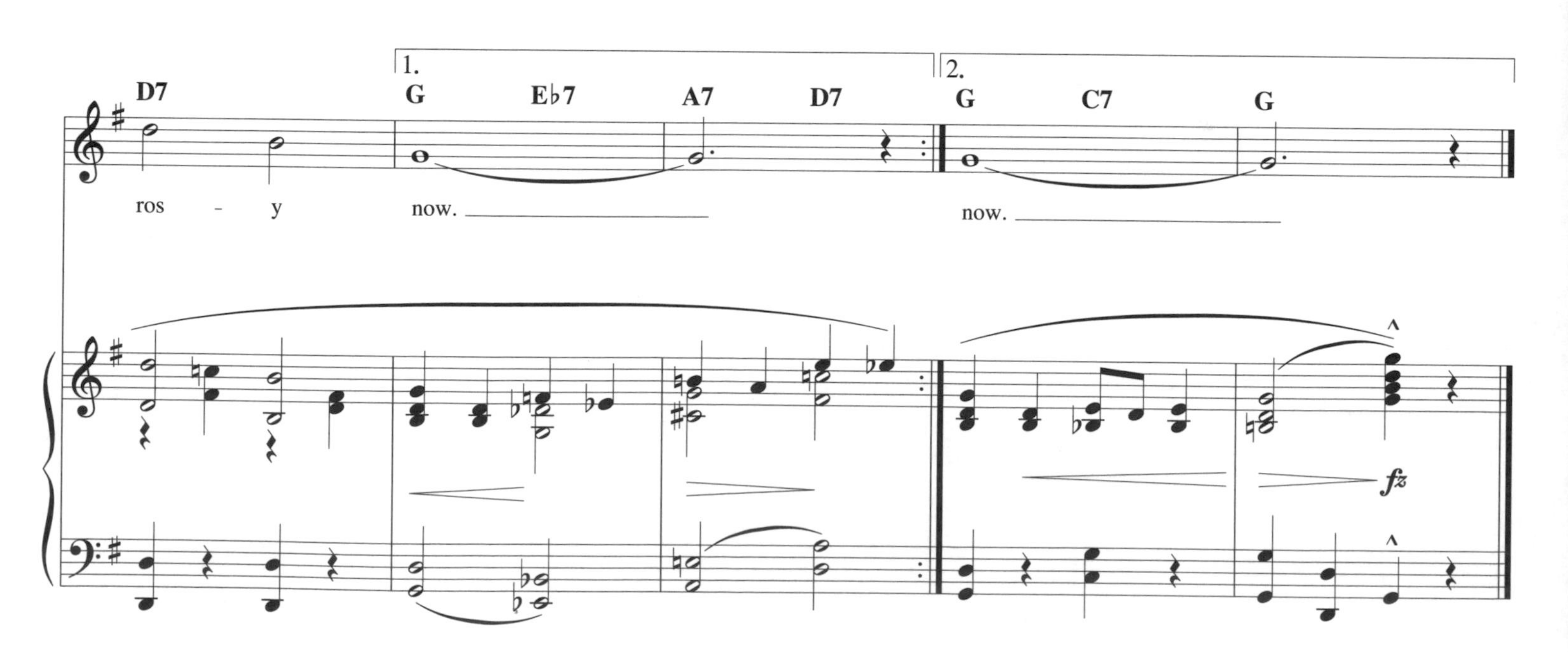
D7
1.
G
E♭7
A7
D7
2.
G
C7
G
ros - y now.
now.
fz

No One Ever Tells You

Lyric by Carroll Coates
Music by Hub Atwood

Slow blues
Eb E9 Eb E9 Eb E9
No one ev - er tells you what it's
p
mp - mf
Eb E9 Eb Bbm7/F Gm7 Cm7 Bbm7 A7(#5)
like to love and lose, how it feels to wak - en and have break - fast with the blues,
Ab Adim7 Eb6/Bb Gm7 C7(b9 b5) F7 Cm7 F7
how to go on liv - ing, how to face an - oth - er day. No one ev - er tells you the way.
Db7 F7 B7 Bb7 Eb E7 Eb E7
No one ev - er tells you how it feels to walk a - lone,

Eb Bbm7/F Gm7 Cm7 Bbm7 A7(#5) Ab Adim7
lis - t'ning for those foot - steps through the ech - o of your own. Sud - den - ly it hits you, all those
Eb Gm7 C7(b9 b5) F7 Bb13 Db7 D7 Eb6
dreams weren't worth a dime, 'cause no one ev - er tells you in time.
Bridge 1 & 2
Bb7(#9 #5) Eb7(b5) F#dim Eb7 Ab9
Long be - fore the ic - y winds of Win - ter, Au - tumn tells the swal - lows time to
Long be - fore our love - boat's torn a - sun - der, we can hear the thun - der of the
Eb Ebmaj7 Eb7 Eb6 Abm6 Eb6 Abm6 Eb6
fly. So, why do we pre - tend? 'til the bit - ter end.
falls! So, why do we go on, sail - in' mad - ly on 'til

F7 Gm7 A♭m6 F7
B♭7 A♭ Gm7 B♭7
E♭ E7
'til it breaks our hearts to say good - bye?
all we had is gone be - yond re - call!
No one ev - er tells you that it's
E♭ E7
E♭maj7 Fm7
Gm7 Cm7 B♭m7 A7(♯5)
just an - oth - er fling.
No one ev - er warns you when your heart be - gins to sing.
A♭ Adim7
E♭/B♭ Gm7 C7(♭9)
F7 B♭13
Some - one tells you lat - er "all is fair in love and war."
But no one ev - er tells you be -
1.
2.
E♭ E7
E♭ C7
F7 B♭13
E♭6 E9 E♭9(♯11)
(♯11)
- fore.
- fore. It nev - er comes eas - y, no, no one ev - er tells you be - fore.

Style

From The Motion Picture "Robin and the 7 Hoods"
(Sung by Frank, Bing & Dean)

Lyric by Sammy Cahn
Music by Jimmy Van Heusen

Moderately
mf

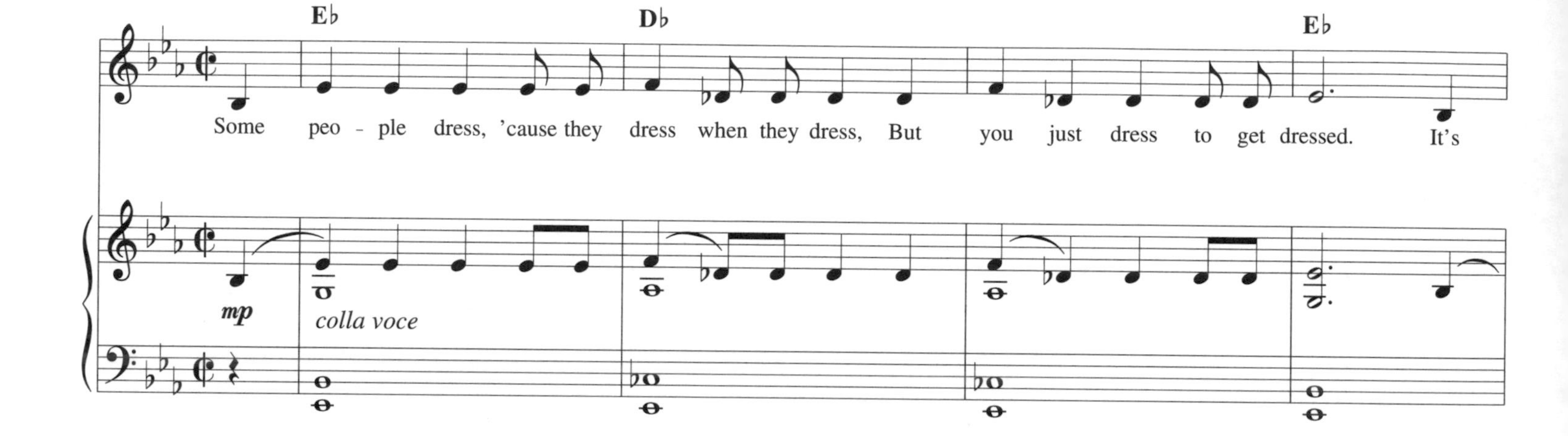
E♭
D♭
E♭
Some peo - ple dress, 'cause they dress when they dress, But you just dress to get dressed. It's
mp
colla voce

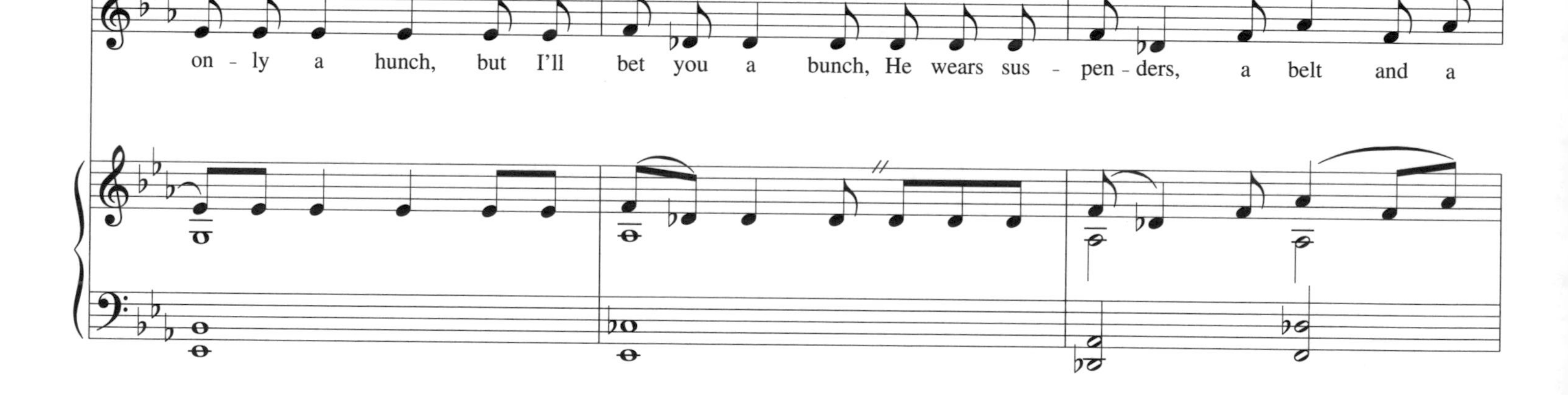
D♭
on - ly a hunch, but I'll bet you a bunch, He wears sus - pen - ders, a belt and a

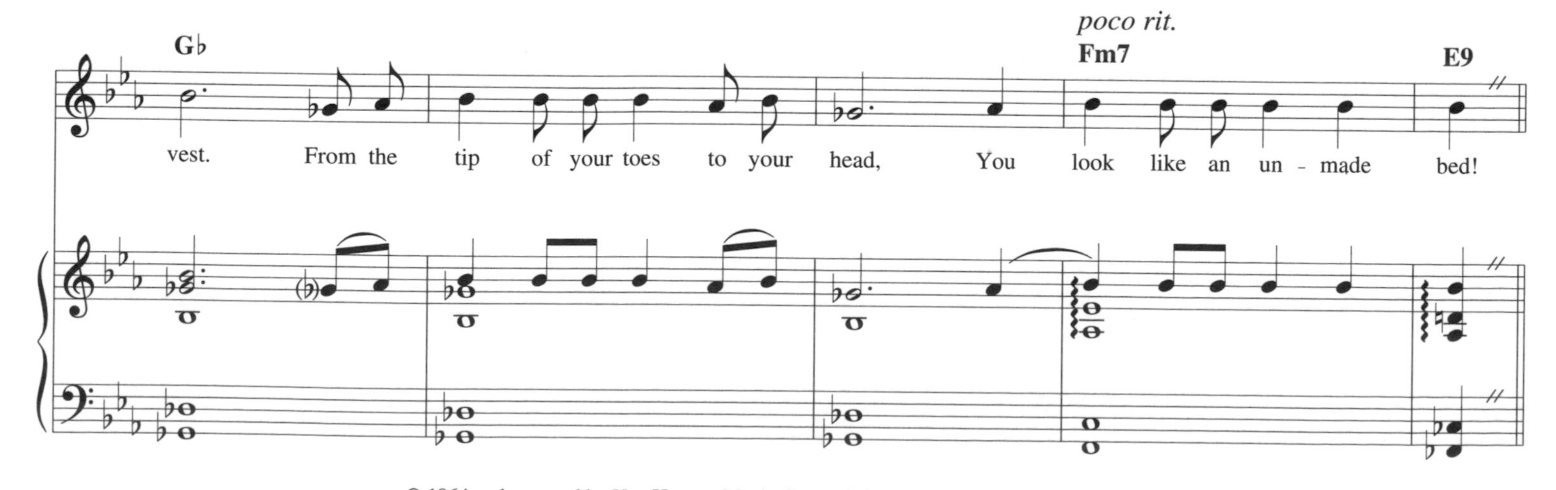
poco rit.
G♭
Fm7
E9
vest. From the tip of your toes to your head, You look like an un - made bed!

Chorus
Moderately
Gm Bb7 Eb6 Gbm6 Bb7 Eb6 Edim
1. You've ei - ther got or you have - n't got style,
2. You've ei - ther got or you have - n't got charm,
3. You've ei - ther got or you have - n't got style,
mf
1. Got or you have - n't got style,
2. Got or you have - n't got charm!
3. Got or you have - n't got style,
Bb9 Eb6 Gm Bb7 Eb Gbm6 Bb7
If you've got it you stand out a
Style and charm sort of go arm in
It's what keeps you a - round for a
Eb6 Edim Bb9 Bbm6 C7 C7+ Fm7
mile! A flow'rs not a
arm! With moth - er of
while! Make sure if the
Got it you stand out a mile!
They kind of go arm in arm!
Keeps you a - round for a while!
Db7 Cm7 F7 Cm7
flow'r if it's wilt - ed, A hat's not a
pearl kind of but - tons, You'll look like the
coat's off the rack, chum, Make sure there's no

F9 Bb9 Gm Bb7 Eb6 Gbm6
hat, 'til it's tilt - ed! You've ei - ther got or you
As - tors and Hut - tons! You've ei - ther got or you
belt in the back, chum! You've ei - ther got or you
Bb7 Eb6 Edim Bb7 Eb6 Gm Bb7
have - n't got class! How it
have - n't got flair! Here's the
have - n't got taste! It's an
Got or you have - n't got class!
Got or you have - n't got flair!
Got or you have - n't got taste!
Eb6 Gbm6 Bb7 Bbm6 C7+
draws the ap - plause of the mass - es! When
plot, flair is what keeps them star - ing! When
art, so be smart and don't waste it! Your
Fm9 Fm7 Db7 Cm7 F7
you wear la - pels like the swell - est of swells, You can
you wear those duds, duds with white tie and studs, Watch those
vest must have scads, scads of wide Scot - tish plaids, And your

Fm7 B♭7 B♭m6 C7 C7+
pass an - y mir - - ror and smile! You've ei - ther
dolls lin - ing up sin - gle file! You've ei - ther
shoes must be real croc - o - - dile! You've ei - ther
Fm7 B♭9 B♭7+ B♭m6 C7
got or you have - n't got, Got or you have - n't got,
got or you have - n't got, Got or you have - n't got,
got or you have - n't got, Got or you have - n't got,
Fm7 B♭9 B♭7+
1., 2.
E♭6 Fm7 B♭9 E♭6
Got or you have - n't got srlye!
Got or you have - n't got style!
Got or you have - n't got
B♭9 Gm B♭7
3.
E♭ B♭7 E♭6
2. You've ei - ther
3. You've ei - ther style!
L.H.

My Kind Of Town

(Chicago Is)

Lyric by Sammy Cahn
Music by James Van Heusen

Cm
Bdim7
B♭m9
A9
G7
all the things Chi - ca - go is to me.
Gee! It's
cresc.
Moderately
A♭
G7
G♭9
F7
F7♭9♯5
my kind of town. Chi - ca - - go is
mf
B♭m
E♭dim7
E♭7
A♭
A♭7
C7♭5
my kind of town. Chi - ca - - go is
D♭6
Ddim7
A♭/E♭
Edim7
Fm
my kind of peo - ple, too,
my kind of razz - ma - tazz,

B♭7
E♭9 E♭dim7 E♭9 G7 A♭
peo - ple who
smile at you. And each
and it has
that there jazz. And each
G7 G♭9 F7 F7♭9♯5 F7 B♭m
time I roam, Chi - ca - go is call - ing me home.
time I leave, Chi - ca - go is tug - ging my sleeve.
E♭dim7 E♭7 A♭ A♭7 C7♭5
1.
D♭6
Chi - ca - go is one
cresc.
Ddim7 A♭/E♭ F7 B♭9
town that won't let you down. It's my
f
Ped.

B♭m7/E♭
E♭7♭9
A♭6
kind of town!
*
B♭m/A♭
A♭dim7
2.
D♭6
Ddim7
mf
This is the Wrig - ley
A♭/E♭
A♭
C7♭5
D♭6
Ddim7
Build - ing, Chi - ca - go is the Wind - - y
A♭/E♭
A♭
C7♭5
D♭6
Ddim7
Cit - y, Chi - ca - go is the Un - - ion

A♭/E♭ A♭ C7♭5 D♭6 Ddim7
Stock - yards, Chi - ca - go is Com - - - - is - - key
A♭/E♭ A♭ C7♭5 D♭6 Ddim7
Ball - park, Chi - ca - go is one town that
cresc.
A♭/E♭ F7 B♭9 B♭m7/E♭
won't let you down. It's my kind
f
E♭7♭9 A♭6 E♭9 A♭6/9
of town!

There Will Never Be Another You

Lyric by Mack Gordon
Music by Harry Warren

F7
Ab m6/Cb
Bb7
Eb
want you to know:
There will be man - y
oth - er nights like this,
Dm7
G7
Cm7
and I'll be stand - ing
here with some - one new.
Bbm7
Eb7
Ab
There will be oth - er
Abm6
Eb
Cm
F7
songs to sing, an - oth - er fall, an - oth - er spring, but there will nev - er

Fm7/B♭ B♭7 E♭
be an - oth - er you. There will be oth - er lips that I may
Dm7 G7 Cm7 B♭m7
kiss, but they won't thrill me like yours used to do.
E♭7 A♭ A♭m6 E♭ G7 Cm F7sus F7 F7♭9
Yes, I may dream a mil - lion dreams, but how can they come true, if
E♭ D7 B♭7 E♭7 Fm7 B♭7sus B♭7 1. E♭ 2. E♭
there will nev - er ev - er be an - oth - er you? There you?
L. H.

Without A Song

Lyric by Billy Rose and Edward Eliscu
Music by Vincent Youmans

Slow
rall.
mf
dim.

Fmaj7
B♭maj7/F
With - out a song the day would nev - er end; with - out a
p

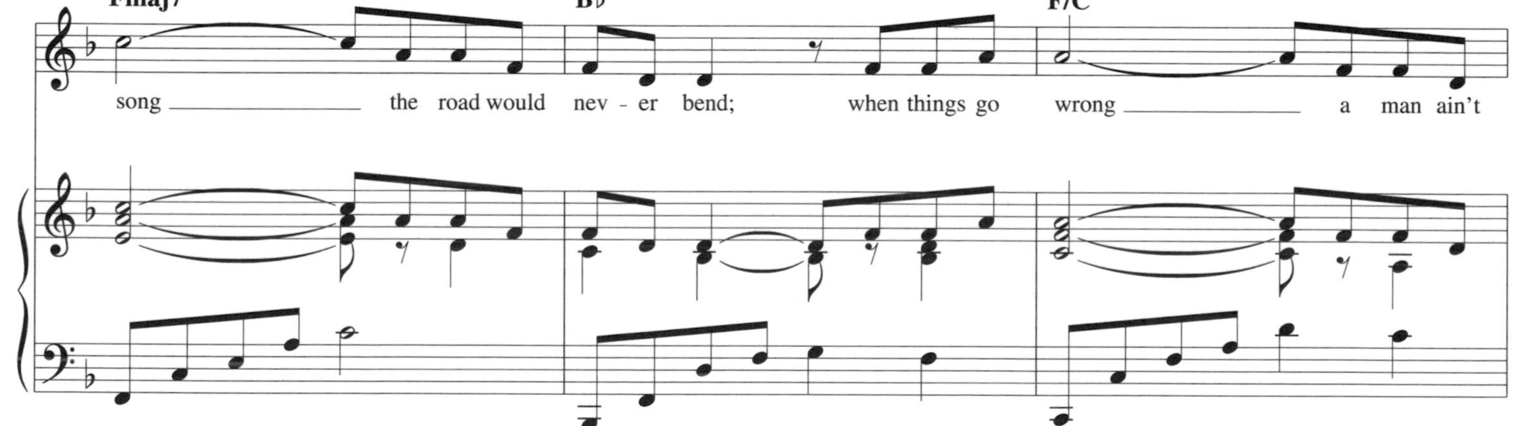
Fmaj7
B♭
F/C
song the road would nev - er bend; when things go wrong a man ain't

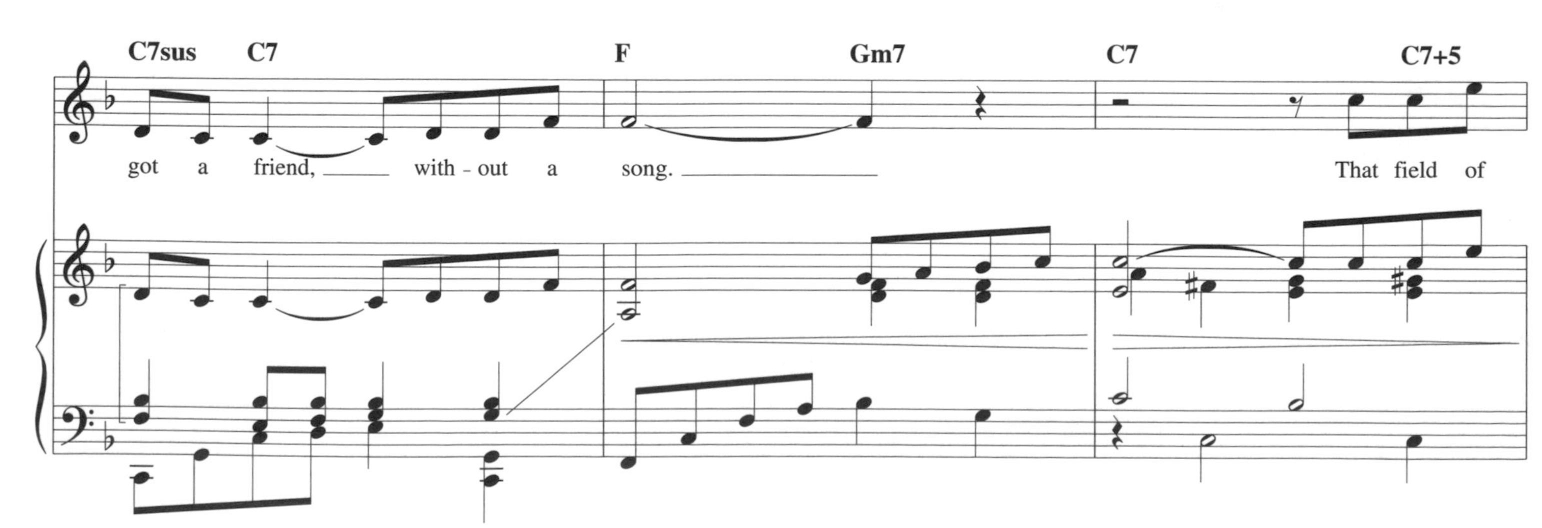
C7sus
C7
F
Gm7
C7
C7+5
got a friend, with - out a song. That field of

Fmaj7
B♭maj7/F
Fmaj7
corn would nev - er see a plow; that field of corn would be de -
B♭
F/C
C7sus
C7
- sert - ed now; a man is born, but he's no good no - how, with out a
F
F7
B♭
F7
B♭
song. I got my trou - ble and woe, but
mf
F7
B♭
F7
B♭
C
F
sure as I know the Jor - dan will roll.

Am E7 Am7 D7 C G7 C F C9
I'll get a - long as long as a song is strong in my soul.
f
ff
C7 C7+5 Fmaj7 B♭maj7/F
I'll nev - er know what makes the rain to fall; I'll nev - er
p
Fmaj7 B♭ F/C
know what makes the grass so tall; I on - ly know there ain't no
C7sus C7 rit. F G7 B♭m F
love at all with - out a song.
cresc.

What Now My Love

(French Title: "Et Maintenant"))

English Lyric by Carl Sigman
French Lyric by Perre Leroyer
Music by Gilbert Becaud

Moderate bolero tempo

R. H.
L. H.

Gm7
F
B♭6
F6
What now my love Now that you left me How can I
love Now that it's o - ver I feel the
Et main - te - nant que vais - je fai - re De tout ce
nant que vais - je fai - re Vers quel né -

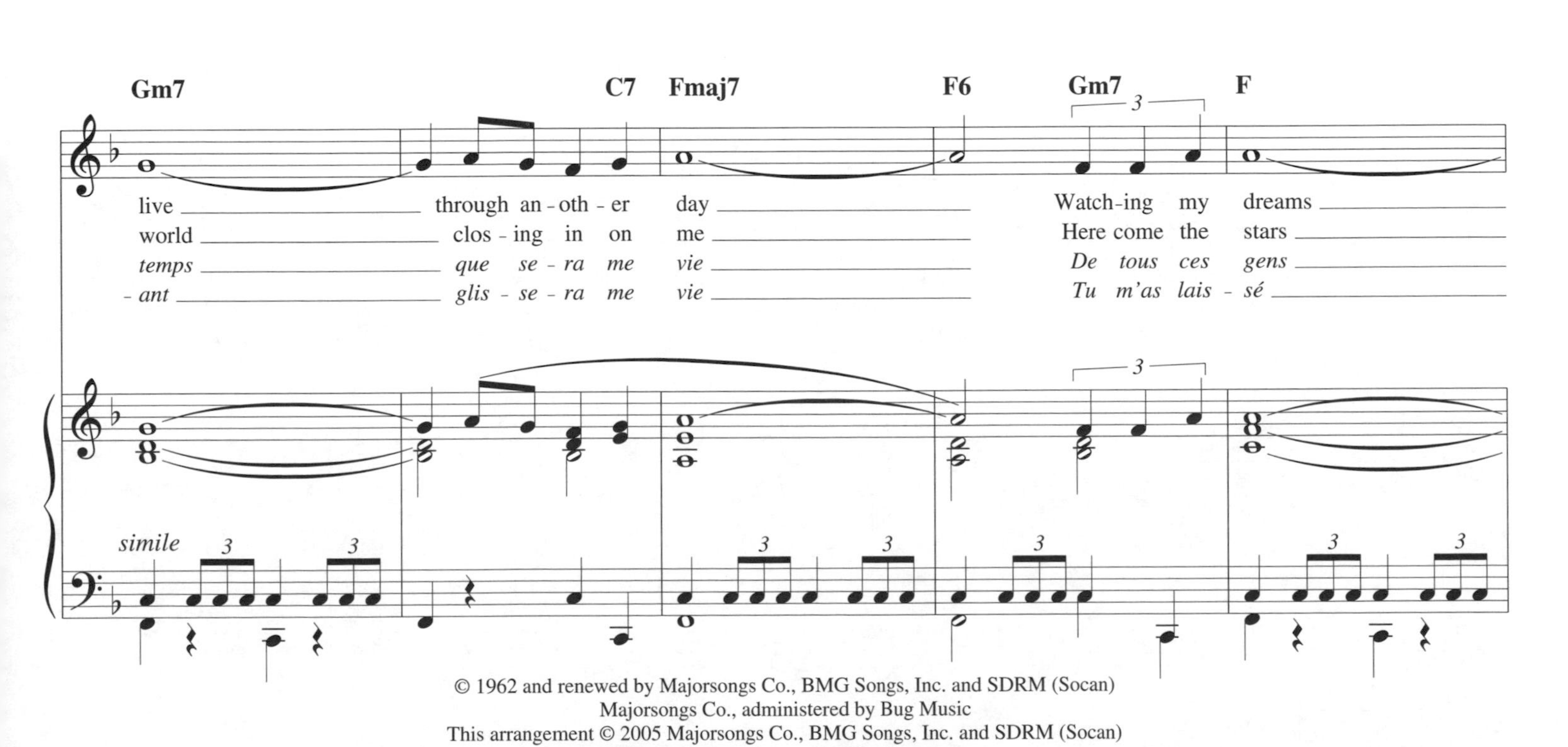
Gm7
C7
Fmaj7
F6
Gm7
F
live through an - oth - er day Watch-ing my dreams
world clos - ing in on me Here come the stars
temps que se - ra me vie De tous ces gens
- ant glis - se - ra me vie Tu m'as lais - sé
simile

B♭6 F6 Gm7 C7
Turn-ing to ash - es And my hopes in - to bits of
Tum-bling a - round me There's the sky where the sea should
qui m'in-dif - fe - rent Main - te - nant que tu es par -
la terre en - tiè - re Mais la terre sans toi c'est pe -
F Fmaj7 F7 Gm7 C7 Am7
clay Once I could see Once I could feel
be What now my love Now that you're gone
- tie Tou - tes ces nuits pour-quoi, pour qui
- tit Vous mes a - mis soy - es gen - tils
Dm7 Gm7 C7 Gm7 C7 F Fmaj7 F7
Now I am numb I've be-come un - real I walk the
I'd be a fool to go on and on No one would
Et ce ma - tin qui re - vient pour rien Mon coeur qui
Vous sa - vez bien que l'on n'y peut rien Mè - me Pa -

B♭m7 E♭7 A♭maj7 D♭maj7 D♭6 B♭m6
night With-out a goal Stripped of my heart,
care No one would cry If I should live
bat pour qui, pour - quoi Qui bat trop fort,
- ris cre - ve d'en - nui Tou - tes ces rues
Bdim Gm7/C C7 Gm7 C7 Gm7
my soul. What now my What now my
or die.
trop fort. Et main - te - Je n'ai vrai -
me tuent.
F B♭6 F6 Gm7
love Now there is noth - ing Only my last
- ment plus rien a fai - re Je n'ai vrai - ment
simile
Gm7 C9 Fmaj7 F6 Fmaj7 F6
good - bye.
plus rien.

Moonlight in Vermont

Lyric by John Blackburn
Music by Karl Suessdorf

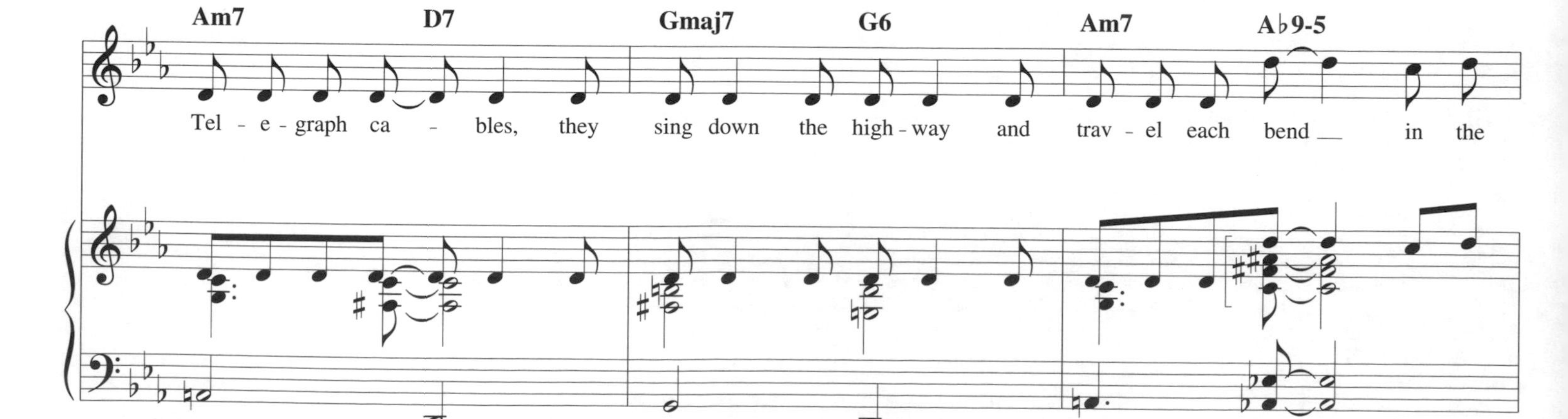

Gmaj G6 B♭m7 E♭7 A♭maj7 A♭6
road, Peo - ple who meet __ in this ro - man - tic set - ting are
B♭m7 E♭9 A♭ B♭7+ E♭ E♭maj7 Fm7 E7
so hyp - no - tized __ by the love - ly ev' - ning sum - mer breeze,
E♭ Cm D♭9 Fm B♭7 E♭
warb - ling of a mea - dow - lark, moon - light in Ver - mont,
1. 2.
F9 E9 E♭ B♭9 B♭9+ E♭
You and I and moon - light in Ver - mont - mont.

Selected Discography

The many classic songs in this book have been recorded by hundreds of great performers in many different styles over the years. Listed below are just a few of the favorite CD Recordings chosen by our staff for you to consider. In most cases we have tried to list the original album title, however all of them appear on reissue compilations as well.

All Of Me
Frank Sinatra "Songs For Young Lovers/Swing Easy"
Billie Holiday "Lady In Autumn"
John Pizzarelli "All Of Me"

Chicago
Frank Sinatra "Come Fly With Me" Expanded Edition
Judy Garland "Judy At Carnegie Hall"
Tony Bennett & Count Basie "Basie Swings/Bennett Sings"

A Day In The Life Of A Fool
Frank Sinatra "My Way"
Monica Mancini "Cinema Paradiso"
Jack Jones "Greatest Hits"

Don't Take Your Love From Me
Frank Sinatra "Greatest Love Songs " Ballad Version
Frank Sinatra "Come Swing With Me" Swing Version
Keely Smith "I Wish You Love"

Everybody Has The Right To Be Wrong!
Frank Sinatra "My Kind Of Broadway"
Julie Harris "Skyscraper Original Cast"
Bobby Darin "In A Broadway Bag"

How Little We Know (How Little It Matters)
Frank Sinatra "Sinatra's Sinatra"
Carmen McRae "Here To Stay"
Chris Conner "I Miss You So/Witchcraft"

I'm Gonna Live Till I Die
Frank Sinatra "Complete Capitol Singles"
Sarah Vaughan "A Touch Of Class"
Frankie Lane "The Frankie Lane Collection"

Isle Of Capri
Frank Sinatra "Come Fly With Me"
Rosemary Clooney/Bing Crosby "Fancy Meeting You Here"
Tommy Edwards "The Best Of Tommy Edwards"

It Was A Very Good Year
Frank Sinatra "September Of My Years"
Ray Charles "Genus Loves Company"
Lou Rawls "Soulin"

The Last Dance
Frank Sinatra "Come Dance With Me"
Rosemary Clooney "Sings Jimmy Van Heusen"
Rebecca Kilgore "The Music Of Jimmy Van Heusen"

The Lonesome Road
Frank Sinatra "A Swingin' Affair"
Anita O'Day "Giants Of Jazz"
June Christy "This Is June Christy"

Looking At The World Thru Rose Colored Glasses
Frank Sinatra "Sinatra & Basie"
Allan Harris "Here Comes Allan Harris"
Frank Sinatra "Complete Reprise Studio Sessions"

Moonlight In Vermont
Frank Sinatra "Come Fly With Me"
Ella Fitzgerald "Hello Love"
Mel Torme "20th Century Masters"

My Blue Heaven
Frank Sinatra "Sinatra's Swingin' Session"
Carol Sloan "The Real Thing"
John Pizzarelli "My Blue Heaven"

My Kind Of Town
Frank Sinatra "The Reprise Collection
Julie London "Love Letters/Feeling Good"
Jack Jones "My Kind Of Town"

No One Ever Tells You
Frank Sinatra "A Swingin' Affair"
Diane Schuur & B B King "Heart Of Hearts"
Rebecca Paris "Love Comes And Goes"

Style
Frank Sinatra, Bing Crosby & Dean Martin
from the Motion Picture "Robin & The Seven Hoods
Frank Sinatra "Complete Reprise Studio Sessions"

What Now My Love?
Frank Sinatra "That's Life"
Nancy Wilson "The Ultimate Collection"
Elvis Presley "Aloha From Hawaii"

Without A Song
Frank Sinatra "My Kind Of Broadway"
Tierney Sutton "Dancing In The Dark"
Tony Bennett & Count Basie "In Person"

Music notation by Forte Music / Cover design by Design Concepts